# A Westie's Song
Bramble, Bruce & Wee Jack

Copyright © 2024 J.R. Bates

All rights reserved.

A Westie's Song: Bruce, Bramble & Wee Jack

No part of this book may be reproduced, stored in a retrieval system, or transmitted in any form or by any means—electronic, mechanical, photocopying, recording, or otherwise—without prior written permission from the publisher, except in the case of brief quotations embodied in critical articles and reviews.

This is a work of fiction. Any resemblance to actual events, locales, or persons, living or dead, is entirely coincidental. The opinions expressed are those of the author and do not necessarily reflect those of the publisher.

**Publisher:**

J.R. Bates

www.jrbates-author.co.uk

**ISBNs:**

eBook: 978-1-80541-675-3

Paperback: 978-1-80541-676-0

First edition, 2024

**Disclaimer:**

This book contains a blend of imaginative storytelling and satire, including commentary on societal and political issues, intended for entertainment and thoughtful reflection.

# A Westie's Song

## Bramble, Bruce & Wee Jack

J.R. Bates

# TABLE OF CONTENTS

| CHAPTER ONE | **GOODBYE/HELLO** | 1 |
| CHAPTER TWO | **FIRST DAY LESSONS** | 17 |
| CHAPTER THREE | **HUMANS ARE FUNNY ANIMALS** | 25 |
| CHAPTER FOUR | **HOLIDAY INDEED** | 33 |
| CHAPTER FIVE | **A PLACE CALLED ROGART** | 47 |
| CHAPTER SIX | **BRAMBLE LIFE-GUARD** | 57 |
| CHAPTER SEVEN | **JACK IN THE BOX** | 65 |
| CHAPTER EIGHT | **GOODBYE FOLKS** | 75 |
| **WEE JACK'S POSTSCRIPT (BY HIS DAD)** | | 77 |
| THE END | **'AS IF'** | 79 |
| BRUCE AND JACK | **SLEEPY BROTHERS** | 81 |
| DAD'S POEM | **GIVE A DOG A BAD NAME** | 87 |
| **ACKNOWLEDGEMENTS** | | 91 |

Hi folks, I realise that some of you who are taking the time to read this preamble to my memoir... in all probability, and quite understandably aren't ready for a book about dogs... and authored by a dog. If that is the case, then read no further and return to your elves and pixies, quidditch and weird railway stations, for they are interesting too. If, however, you can unleash your mind and accept an offering from our oft abused but forgiving animal kingdom, then read on... for this is it, my book, or my Westie attempt at it.

I appreciate that canine-phobia is rampant in the UK and English-speaking world because of the widely held belief that any life form with four legs and a hairy body with the inability to communicate verbally must be thick and stupid. Not so, human people... it's a complete misunderstanding... we're actually more advanced than you think. My human family taught me those things... and they taught me about the disparity between talk and action. The huge political promises and the disappointing results. I point you to the Trumps, Johnsons and Putins of this world to allow you to draw your own comparisons. Who indeed is on a higher plane... and who should be classified as lesser life?

To be fair, that same attitude is not so rampant in other parts of the world because we're a non-entity... a commodity and an afterthought. In many places basically, we're food, and actually a delicacy in parts of China, and areas of Russia and the far east... how disgusting is that?... because it would never cross my mind to eat human flesh. Myself and my kind are far more advanced than that. We believe all life is sacred... 'don't you?'

I actually have a story to tell you. It's my story, and it may not be fantastic or violent enough for you. I have to admit that I once chased a rabbit and killed it... and my human mam was terribly upset so I never did it again. After that I still used to bark at the little buggers and warn them off... and I even chased them, but I never took the life of a rabbit ever again.

This tale may not be on Netflix or Amazon for murders are at a premium, no superheroes or alien invaders and not a single fairy, elf or wand, but at least it will be true and not fantasy. This is my story, my life story... it's as I remember it, and as true as I can make it while my last hours play out in the arms of my human mam and dad. This is my song... my Westie song... I hope you like it.

# CHAPTER ONE
# GOODBYE/HELLO

So, here I am, a West Highland white terrier or so I've been reliably informed, and I'm sitting in a big brick pen with all my brothers and sisters. The humans call this time February 2008 and they tell me I'm six weeks old now. But the truth is I'm really sad because I haven't seen my mam for over a week and I miss her scent terribly. The last seven days have been awful and I've had a little cry and a whine to myself on a night-time... but it hasn't helped and she hasn't re-appeared. I know she's okay because I can hear her and smell her, so she must be close, but the humans aren't letting us puppies be with her. Apparently it's all part of the separation process... but what do I know?

All I know for sure is that I'm not having mam's milk anymore and I'm having to eat some disgusting sloppy porridge mess out of a dish on the floor. I don't like it at all and can't be bothered to fight with my siblings to get at the yucky offering when feeding-time comes around. This lack of fight has prompted the boss human who is in charge of us

Westies to give me my official name... he says I'm 'Runt of the Litter'... and that makes me very proud because none of my brothers and sisters have official names yet. So, I'm not 'Sniff 7' anymore. I must be a very special Westie indeed.

Yesterday 'Sniff 6', my brother, left us to go off with his new family and educate some humans. Unlike me, he hadn't been given a name before he left and we just recognised each other as 'Sniff 6' and 'Sniff 7'. We said our goodbyes just before he was taken away. Our boss human lifted him out of the pen and handed him over to a woman person... his new mother to be.

'Hello Hamish... you look like a Hamish,' the woman took hold of my brother gently, then she snuggled him into her bust and gave him a human kiss on top of his head. She seemed nice and in desperate need of some doggy affection. 'Welcome to our family you little darling.' The lady had tears in her eyes. Sniff 6 looked over to me and head-winked... he looked happy... he'd certainly fallen on his paws. I winked back and sent him his final thought message, *see you around brother*, then in a blink of an eye he was gone.

As for the thought message thing... we Westies, and all other dogs too... or so I believe, communicate with scent first of all, then we use dog telepathy... talking to each other in dog-speak, head-to-head, no barks or words needed. Thoughts and emotions go from one head to another and we understand it... it's simple and we're born with it, and it's much better than the human alternative. I was soon to find out that humans don't have this ability and they can only communicate with a complicated mish-mash of hand gestures, face pulling, and barky noises that they call chatting... how complicated is that? And in all of my almost fourteen years I've never once seen two humans sniffing each other.

My other siblings were 'Sniff 1' my brother, and he was the real tough pup of the litter; then 'Sniff 2, 3 and 4' were my sisters, and finally 'Sniff 5' who was also my brother but like me he wasn't tough, and I worried about him... a lot. He was scrawny like me and there was something wrong. He'd told me a few times that he felt poorly. I'd sniffed his bum and that told me he wasn't kidding... he was indeed poorly but I couldn't make the big human man understand. The very night before I left to join up with my own adopted humans I cuddled into 'Sniff 5' and that made him happy.

Night quickly became morning and I certainly wasn't expecting to be next to leave on that particular day. I was the 'special one' after all, and one of my sisters told me that she'd heard humans always save the best till last, so I reckoned that being 'runt of the litter' would definitely mean that I was the last to be picked. Maybe boss human would even think about letting me stay here with mam.

Good news though. Very early in the morning, while it was still dark outside and even before the stinky porridge was served up, a big human with a funny hat came to see my brother 'Sniff 5'. He had a big box with him and a long tube around his neck. At the top of the tube were two funny white things and he put these into his ears before using the bottom bit of the tube to press on my brother's chest. I was surprised because my brother didn't wriggle or anything... I'm sure I would have. Then the big human shone a little light into 'Sniff 5s' eyes, pulled his lip up to look into his mouth and then turned him around, lifted his tail and poked a little silver tube up his bum. After a few seconds he took it out, shook it, then gave it a hard stare before smiling. I wasn't pleased when he smiled because I certainly didn't think it was funny.

I was sitting as far away as I could and kept my bum hard to the floor in case he came for me with his silver tube, but he didn't. Instead he filled a different tube with some milky liquid and squirted it into my brother's mouth. Then he took out another tube with a sharp skinny spike on the end... then pushed the spike into my brother's haunch and squeezed the top end of the tube. I had to look away but my brother didn't flinch at all; I thought he was being very brave.

Then the funny hat human went to talk to our regular boss human and they barked at each other before doing that smile thing and shaking paws. Our boss human picked up my brother and took him away into the place where he lived in his own kennel with his human bitch and puppies. I didn't know what had just happened but I had a feeling that it could be something good.

Indeed it was something good. Before the day was half-way through, who should be placed gently back in our pen but 'Sniff 5'. He was bouncing about like a mad thing and jumping all over us. The humans had made him better. One of my sisters told him off about the jumping, she even gave him a nip but to no avail, he was just happy to be back with his family again. I bounced over to see him and I asked him if he was alright. For an answer he jumped on my back and we rolled around on the floor for a while having a play fight. He was so happy that day and I was happy too... so I let '5' win.

Dogs can't smile like humans but he gave me a head grin and told me he was feeling on top of the world. All the humans in their big kennel had been making a fuss of him and he'd slept on a blanket in front of a big fire. One of the human puppies had stayed with him and gave him some big cuddles until the white medicine worked. Then when he was feeling better they gave him a big dish of special food... not porridge, and another squirt of milky medicine. I was pleased for my brother, and it gave me a much different opinion of the big human who looked after us... he was alright.

Food came next and I was starving so I had a few mouthfuls of the awful gruel but that was as much as I could manage before feeling queasy. I'd even given some thought to pretending to be poorly so that I could have some of that nice food in the human kennel but honestly I couldn't be bothered. I knew that soon I'd be exchanged for lots of sheets of human money paper before going off with some sad two-legged person who was desperately in need of some Westie therapy. That was my job and our mission in life... to make sad humans happy... or so mam had told all of us puppies.

Then it happened... the meeting that was to change my life. I hadn't made any plans for this... how could I?... I was a puppy for heaven's sake and I'm looking back at those days with all the information that I have now as a fourteen-year-old. Back then I was just a normal mad-head pup who didn't even know how to scratch at the door when I needed a poo... I just did what I had to do whenever I felt the need... and then let the daft human folk clean up after me... that's what was meant to happen, wasn't it?

On that eventful morning the first time I saw my human mam and dad I wasn't impressed. Mam looked friendly enough, but dad... or the man who was to be my new dad looked like a total grouch. He didn't even smile when he was talking to our boss human, and he had an older male Westie with him on a lead. To be honest that Westie looked even grumpier than the man and it seemed like he wanted to be anywhere but here. I immediately understood the situation and tucked myself away in the furthest corner, as far away from the speculative parents as I could manage. I tried to look anywhere but at those two humans. These people were nothing like my real mam... they didn't have enough hair or legs and they smelt funny, but I was intelligent enough to understand that like it or not two-legged folk like this were to be a big part of my future.

I'd heard all kinds of stories from Gizmo... our boss human's dog when he sneaked in to frighten us pups with his terrifying stories... but I knew he was just showing off, or at least I thought I did. Because if all his stories were correct about dogs that he knew... who were being kicked and bashed with sticks, starved and left out in the cold and rain, then how come Gizmo had such a shiny coat and a nice bed?

Not only that but he also went out for walks and holidays and got to eat really nice food with chunks of meat in it... so his stories just didn't ring true as far as I was concerned.

So, on that particular day I reckoned it must be time for one of my sisters or perhaps my brother 'Sniff 5' to find their new human family to supply with joy. I watched out of the corner of my eye with interest as the human lady moved around the outside of our enclosure. Like typical madcaps two of my sisters ran up to the wall where the lady was standing and tried to clamber up but it was too high. The lady reached over, smiling, and stroked them but for some reason she had her eyes fixed on me... or possibly '5' who was crouched quite close by. She did one of those people gesture things to our regular boss human and pointed towards me... and it was definitely me. I pretended to be uninterested. This lady obviously wasn't aware that I was special... the 'runt of the litter' and because of that I should be the last to go... who did she think she was? Then I thought to myself... *maybe she's special too and that's why she's recognised me. She must be important.*

She was important... and so was my new dad, extremely important. I didn't realise it at that moment but they were about to give me a life that many of my dog friends and family could only dream of. A life full, not of things or fancy houses and cars, or designer collars with shiny diamonds... or any of the other possessions that humans hold dear... but a life full of love and cuddles, vet appointments and walks in the countryside, fun and games in the back garden and on the beach... and total devotion. I was meeting a human family for the first time, but if any of my canine peers have had a better life then I congratulate them because I couldn't imagine how life with my human family could have ever been improved. Mam and dad I love you both.

Okay, enough of the soppy talk. Anyhow on that fateful day I realised what was coming when I was picked up by our regular human, quite gently as it happened, and I swiftly sent my telepathy goodbyes to my brother and sisters. I heard all of them reply and one of my sisters was crying. Then I was put into the arms of my new mam. I was frightened at first but she smelt nice and she cuddled me in and stroked my head. I relaxed too quickly and had a wee. I was embarrassed and thought that maybe she'd put me down after my little mistake and pick one of my sisters instead. But she didn't.

'Oh you little rascal Bruce,' my new mam chuckled and smiled as she held me in one hand and dabbed at the wet patch on her blouse with a paper tissue. 'That was a lovely greeting little man.'

*My name's not Bruce,* I head shouted, trying to get those thoughts out of my head and into hers, but I couldn't, her head was closed off and I couldn't find a way in, *My name's Runt... Runt of the Litter... honestly, it's the truth, just ask the boss human... he knows.*

Regular boss human didn't say a word. He could have corrected her but instead he was busy counting through a pile of money paper that new dad had put in his hand. When the counting finished he put a bigger piece of paper in new dad's hand and said, 'That's the pedigree and registration...

and I'd advise you to take out insurance as soon as possible.'

New dad paused and thought hard for a few seconds, 'Why is that?... he's not the runt of the litter is he?'

'Nah, of course not the runt went yesterday for half price. It's always best to have insurance for your dog... is all I meant.'

New dad seemed satisfied with that but I was desperately head shouting, *Eeeh, you big liar, tell him the truth... you know I'm 'Runt of the Litter'... let new dad know that I'm special... 'new dad', 'new dad', it's me... Runt, don't believe that liar. You're lucky new dad, you've got the special one.*

Regular human turned away with his bundle of paper and didn't say a word. He didn't tell them the truth and I was disappointed because he didn't even come over and say goodbye to me... or even let me say goodbye to mam... perhaps he wasn't alright after all.

Thirty minutes later and I'm on the long back seat of a car. New dad was driving and new mam was sitting between two Westies. Myself to her left in a little basket with a nice soft pillow and a cuddly blanket that had little dog pictures all over it. Before we'd left she had fastened a little blue tartan collar around my neck and I thought it made me look special. To her right was the older westie she called Bramble and he was lying at new mam's side with his head on her lap, a red tartan collar around his neck, and he was staring hard at me. I don't think he was too impressed with the new addition to his family. I tried not to look back at him.

The journey was long and awful: I was sick twice, poo'd

once and wee'd lots of times. I was really frightened and started to cry but new-mam cuddled me in and made some nice noises. They were sounds without words which I'd later find out were called lullabies. New dad was being grumpy in the front because he must have been tired. We were driving from near Aberdeen to my new home beside a place called Tain. It was an awfully long way and he'd already had to drive that same journey in reverse.

We stopped several times for a rest and a wander around outside… 'to stretch the legs' I heard new dad say and at each stop mam gave me a dish with some milk in and some nice tasting porridge, nothing like the awful porridge at my puppy home. The other Westie, Bramble, gobbled some meaty strip things and only drank water but he kept well away from me and seemed annoyed at having to share his mam and dad. Only once during one of our stops did he bother to give me a sniff and for a brief second he allowed me to sniff back… but he wasn't happy. Maybe he was insecure… but that was no excuse, at least he could have said 'hello' to me or something.

One funny thing though was that whenever we stopped for a rest, new dad would get out of the car then lean back against the closed door and put a white stick into his mouth. Using his paws he would make some fire come out of a little silver machine he'd taken out of his pocket. Then he would put the fire up to the white stick and give it a big suck. After a few seconds he would blow stinky grey clouds out of his mouth and go 'Aahh… that's better.' I think he was just showing off, but I was really impressed.

It seemed a long, long time before we arrived at my new home. It was called Northwilds cottage and it was in the middle of nowhere. I'd fallen asleep a few times in the car and I remember I had some awful dreams. *What if Gizmo had been telling the truth about the awful cruel humans. And what if this new mam and dad were just pretending to be nice before they started with the stick hitting stuff.* But every time I woke up mam would give me a cuddle and do the lullaby noises... and she smelt nice apart from where I'd had a wee on her blouse... so I felt safe.

When the car finally stopped, and our journey was over I was really scared because it was pitch black... I couldn't see anything except the stars up in the sky, and it was so cold and icy. New dad got out of the car first but this time he didn't do the stick in the mouth routine. He moved away into the dark and made some rattly noises with some long shiny things he took out of his pocket. I think he called them keys and they were for opening the house door. A few moments later a light came on, a really big one, and it shone brightly on the outside of the place they called home.

New mam waited with me in the car until new dad returned. He opened the rear door at Bramble's side first and lifted him out of the car before putting him gently down on the ground. Bramble didn't wait around in the cold, he ran straight into the cottage through the newly opened door. Then new dad came around to my side of the car, opened the door and picked up the little basket with me inside it. 'Time to see your new home little fella,' and with that he carried me into my forever place. Maybe new dad wasn't so grouchy after all. Mam took her time to gather together all the accumulated rubbish before closing the car doors and following along behind.

That first night in the cottage put all my fears to rest. I was really hungry and thirsty and human mam made some really lovely food. I gobbled it down quickly and then sneaked across to Bramble's bowl to see if there was any more. Bramble warned me off... then did a head speak with me for the first time. *You can't have the same as me Bruce. You're not old enough for grown-up food so don't even think about nicking any from my bowl or else you'll have me to deal with.* That sounded ominous and Bramble looked a lot tougher than even 'Sniff 1' so I backed away and lay down. But I wasn't happy with the name thing that they were calling me.

I was only little but I wasn't having that... they needed to know my official name because the Boss human hadn't bothered telling them.

*You should call me by my proper name... it's Runt of the Litter. I'm not called Bruce,* I head-shouted, *Why can't you all call me by my proper name?* I protested. I would have stamped my foot if I'd known how.

*Don't be so stupid,* growled Bramble. *Runt of the Litter is a silly thing that humans say to each other and it means you were the weakest of the puppies. You were the one they wanted to get rid of, and that man was just being awful to you. So don't ever let mam and dad know... they're nice parents and they would be upset if they ever found out.* Then he gave me a long hard stare, *and another thing... never let mam and dad know that you can understand human talk... okay? I'll tell you why tomorrow when we're outside.* Bramble gave me a long hard stare then left it at that and wandered over to lie down in front of the fire that new dad was setting.

Mam came through into the front room with a big damp cloth and some disinfectant and began rubbing at the carpet where I'd done a wee. Then she went to the back door that led into the garden and she put down a white pad just inside the exit. Something was going on, something special but I wasn't frightened anymore, I knew these humans were alright. New mam came and picked me up and carried me to the pad and set me down on it. It smelled funny and it made me want to wee again... so I did. Mam clapped her hands and gave my head a rub, 'What a clever boy you are... that was so clever,' then she shouted through into the big room, 'Jim, Jim, he's just had a wee on the puppy pad, come and tell him how clever he is.'

I heard the grumping noise from the front room as the Jim dad roused himself to come through and view my success. He was talking under his breath but my hearing was so much better than theirs and I could hear the words that new mam couldn't. 'Bloody wee on the pad, give him a round of applause, why not put an advert in the flaming paper.' Then new dad appeared. 'Ohhh what a clever boy you are... isn't he a clever boy mam?' Dad wasn't being sarcastic he was just trying to get into new mam's good books.

'He certainly is... he's a little star. I told you he looked like the cleverest of the litter.'

I could hear a snort from Bramble in the front room. He sent me a head thought, *See if you can have a poo as well clever dick and they'll both start cheering, bloody cleverest of the litter indeed.* I did as I was told and had a poo as well. Mam was ecstatic, clapping her hands and scratching my head... just because I'd done a poo, but I'd made her happy. Dad however just grunted... scowled, and walked back the way he had come... I think he was really tired out from driving the car and needed a rest. I wasn't bothered though, I was enjoying this new family experience.

Then it became bedtime and that was a strange affair.

I cried and cried because I was missing my proper mam and my brothers and sisters... I didn't know if I'd ever get to see them again. I was feeling so frightened, even though new mam and dad were really nice... but my new brother 'Bramble' seemed as if he didn't like me at all... and he looked very tough. I was just a bairn and terrified about what the future had in store for me and I couldn't know how it was going to play out. I was desperately in need of some affection.

I got it that night... affection I mean. New mam and dad put me in a cage thing with some blankets and a little bit of material that smelt of my proper mam. They were only being kind, I realise that now, but it made me feel even worse and I just wept like the puppy I was when the light went out. 'Mam... ohhh mam, proper mam please come and cuddle me in... I can smell you and I miss you so much.'

Bramble was lying in his dog bed snuggled into a pile of blankets and he wasn't amused. *Will you shut your whining* and whingeing and let them have some sleep, they've been up since early morning to go and fetch you from that Aberdeen place... and you're crying like a big baby.

I'm frightened Bramble... really frightened, I'm not tough like you... I want my mam.

Bramble seemed pleased with my tough comment and took a little while to have himself a good think, *Okay Bruce... tell you what, give it some really big whines and squeaks and I'll do the rest. I can remember what it was like on my first night... don't worry about it... just do some more crying stuff and I'll tell them to give you a cuddle. I'll fill you in tomorrow on all the human stuff you need to know.*

That was nice of him, he seemed to be warming to me. So I did what he'd told me. I whinged and whined and squeaked for a good ten minutes... and Bramble began to bark... I couldn't understand what his barks were meant to do, it was just dog shouting and it wasn't even proper words but I thought to myself *I'll have to learn them bark things...* because after a few minutes they got results.

'Ohhh for Pete's sake,' I heard new dad growl. 'Will you do something about that noise so I can get some sleep?'

'I can't do anything... apart from bring him up onto the bed. He's frightened, it's not his fault,' said new mam. She was being very diplomatic because looking back on that night... dad was exhausted.

'Put the little fella on the bed then... on your side. I don't want to be cleaning up after him. Just do it Lorraine... I'm shattered.'

Shuffle-shuffle-shuffle... then next thing I knew the door of the cage was being opened and I was in new mam's arms.

'Come on Bruce... you must be missing your doggie mam terribly,' she whispered as she held me close, 'I know I'm not the same... but I'll give you all the love that I can.'

'Lorraine... will you shut up and get into bed for heaven's sake... I really need some sleep,' grumped new dad, 'I'll be walkin' around like a zombie tomorrow if you don't get him settled. I've got that fencing to put up before Ron, Kitty and Shelley arrive.' With that dad turned his back and snuggled down as mam cuddled me in under the fat blanket thing that they called a duvet.

Three times during that first night new mam lifted me out of bed and took me to the puppy pad. Three times I had a wee, and not once... not even once did I have a wee on their bed. I was learning quickly and knew that new dad wouldn't have been pleased if I'd had an accident on their nice duvet. I only cried a little bit because I had someone to cuddle into and pretty soon I was out like a light. My exciting day had caught up with me. I was too tired to even worry about what tomorrow might hold... but I was soon to find out.

# CHAPTER TWO
# FIRST DAY LESSONS

Tomorrow quickly became today... and it turned out to be the first day of my grown-up doggy education. I was just a pup, but I realised that I was going to have to learn quickly, because my teacher... Bramble, was my commanding officer and he wasn't interested in taking prisoners. I had to listen, learn and perform, no questions asked... no excuses accepted.

*Bramble in the snow.*

I discovered quite quickly that Bramble wasn't a monster after all. His name, he informed me, was indeed Bramble... but his title was 'Alpha Male' and it was his job to be top dog and to protect human mam and dad from rabbits and posties. I didn't know what posties were, but Bramble made them sound much more fearsome than rabbits. My name was to be Bruce... no arguments expected, and my title was to be 'wingman' or number two dog. I was to be the 'Val Kilmer' to Bramble's 'Tom Cruise'... and although it took me a while to get the hang of it... it worked.

Bramble opened up to me on that first day and told me why he loved these humans so much. He told me that he'd had three different homes in the three months before he found his forever home. The first one lasted a week because the children in the family found it funny to be cruel to a puppy. The second home was okay but the lady in the family was allergic to dog hair and used to sneeze a lot and struggle to breathe. The third home was back to the lady who had been his first human mam but let him go, and she was old now and couldn't look after him.

So things looked bleak until some lovely people drove from the top end of Scotland down to Dundee... and cuddled Bramble until he'd felt secure. They were mam and dad, or present mam and dad, not at all perfect... but perfect for us because Bramble said that if I made the grade and if I listened and learned then we'd look after them together. That together comment from Bramble really made me feel a part of everything. A family is only as good as its component parts... and I wanted to be one of those.

But boy, I have to tell you, if I'm remembering correctly, that first day was such a laugh... and I honestly wish I hadn't laughed because Bramble was really annoyed with me. On my first sortie outside there were all these white flaky things falling out of the sky and the ground outside was covered in cold stuff they called snow. Mam, who was instantly my protection and first line of defence, wasn't too keen on allowing me outside because it was very chilly... but new dad said, 'We live up the top end of Scotland for heaven's sake... he'll need to get used to it and he'll be fine. We need him to begin socialising with Bramble. Just let him be daft for a while and let him be a pup... we'll keep an eye on them'.

So, the first time I ventured into the back garden I was really nervous. All this space and room to run around, with bushes and fences and empty land as far as the eye could see. I'd been used to snuggling in with my mam in an enclosure with bright lights on the ceiling and just the walls to look at. Now it was like the whole world was waiting for me to make an entrance. All except my new brother Bramble of course.

*What are you laughing at?* was my first head shout from Bramble that day. *What do you find so funny?*

Looking back I have no idea why I head-laughed so hard... but I did. Maybe because Bramble, my big tough brother looked so cute and cuddly. *Ha-ha-ha... you're wearing human clothes... what's that jacket thing you're wearing? You look really stupid.* Bramble was encased in a tartan jacket which went right around his body and fastened underneath his throat and his tummy... he looked like a real poser.

*Stupid... you're calling me stupid?... right, you're in for it now... and I don't care how little you are.* Bramble came running towards me and I knew he was annoyed. I'd made a huge error and now I was terrified. Then Bramble glanced at the window and slowed down, swerving his run so that he went past me.

I looked too and saw mam and dad watching us from the window. *Bruce... do you trust me?* Bramble shouted as he gave me a body swerve. That was a weird head question from my tough new brother, and I didn't dare say anything other than...

*Yes, I suppose so.*

*Good... right answer, you're alright Bruce. So run over to me and jump on my back... I won't hurt you, honest.*

*Ehhh, what for?... you're too big, and you'll bash me one.*

*Because mam and dad are watching us, and they want to know that we're going to be alright together. They need to know that I'm not bullying you. Just do it Bruce I won't bash you or tell you off or anything.*

To be honest I didn't need a second invitation. My little legs began moving sixty to the dozen and I took a flying leap that would have put a human Olympic gymnast to shame. Then 'bash' and I knocked Bramble over into a big pile of snow. Bramble barked and rolled me back over with his body and head-shouted, *Keep going Bruce, mam and dad are laughing.*

They were too. I could see them through the window

out of the corner of my eye. They were watching us with big smiley faces and pointing as we rolled around in the snow stuff. Bramble let me jump all over him and he didn't hurt me or bash me back. He just put up with my antics for a long time, playing chasey with me and letting me win then after a while he slowed everything down and head shouted again, *Okay Bruce, that's enough... calm yourself down and come and give me a lick. Then I'll lick you back and then we'll just walk along together like best pals... down past the shed and the big polytunnel. I'm going to show you where poo-corner is. Don't look back at mam and dad. I don't want them to know we've been putting on a show for them.*

Bramble was being very friendly and it unnerved me somewhat, but I did as I was told and I stopped the pretend fighting. We licked as instructed, had a good old sniff of each other and then we walked together past the tool shed and on towards the big polytunnel where Bramble told me that mam grew some food... things called tomatoes and peppers. It was huge, really huge, and even bigger than my old home... I was impressed.

Then, an even bigger surprise was waiting as we rounded the shed. I couldn't believe my eyes. Out there in the big field were wall-to-wall furry things... zillions of them, and they scattered and ran as soon as they spied Bramble and myself... 'rabbits'... 'yeeha'.

Remember... I was a pup just into my seventh week and I didn't have any instruction as to what I was supposed to do when rabbits appeared, but something deep inside...

and with hindsight probably information passed on from my proper mam told me that I had to chase these furry interlopers... so I did and I shot off like greased lightning. I ignored the head shouts from Bramble... the *No Bruce no, they won't like it... mam will go daft.* He was shouting lots of other things as well about just scaring the bunnies and not biting but it wasn't registering because at that precise moment I had one thought and one thought only... to catch one of the furry buggers, get my chops around it and give it a good head shake. No-one could have stopped me... they would have tried and failed... I was a Westie... a terrier and I had a job to do. I don't know why I knew those things, but I did and I was focussed.

The rabbits scattered in all directions and I was completely engrossed in the thrill of the chase. I ran and ran, jumping over clumps of grass and ploughing through the snow stuff. I was only little, my legs were tired and I was getting out of breath but I kept on running. Then all of a sudden and as if by magic they all seemed to disappear... one moment there were dozens of rushing and leaping rabbits and the next moment they were gone... all but a couple of stragglers.

I was puffing and panting by now but even so I kept going albeit at half speed. Then I came to a halt... even the stragglers had disappeared into thin air. That had me confused... where had they gone? I didn't know at the time that rabbits lived in underground houses. I could still smell those little varmints but they'd vanished from sight. So now completely drained of energy I lay down in the snow. Out there in the field the snow was really deep... over the top of my legs. After a few moments Bramble appeared beside me. He was obviously annoyed because I hadn't listened to him. *Righto smart arse... you've done it now... what did I say about me being Alpha Male and you being my sidekick? Now you're going to find out how tough I really am.*

In that moment I was scared because I knew I'd done something really stupid. I'd ignored my big brother and now Bramble was about to give me a nip... or worse. Just then though salvation arrived and in the nick of time mam and dad appeared from behind the polytunnel; both running, and both looking worried. Next thing that I knew mam had picked me up and wrapped me in a blanket and dad had lifted Bramble up and my brother was much bigger than me. Mam cuddled me in as she walked back towards the cottage. Bramble from dad's arms shouted out a head message, *You ever ignore me again and you're in for it... understand? And if you ever tell any of the other dogs around here that I get picked up and cuddled... you'll be in big trouble.*

I never did mention it to the other dogs from the other remote houses nearest to us; mainly because Bramble would have given me a good pasting, but also because his street cred would have taken a huge hit... and I was actually beginning to warm to my adopted brother.

Back in the house we were picked up then sat on towels on human laps, Bramble on dad's lap and myself on mam's and they were plucking little balls of snow from our legs. Bramble's legs were worse than mine and that must have been because I still had my soft puppy hair. Bramble looked like he had big bunches of white grapes around his paws and up to his knees. It took dad a long time to pick all the snowballs from Bramble's fur and then towel him dry but it didn't faze him one little bit... so I reckoned this must be a regular occurrence. As for myself I squirmed a bit because I didn't know what was happening at first, but mam was really quick and gentle and I was dried and cleaned way before Bramble.

After that episode I followed Bramble wherever he went and I listened whenever he head-talked. Our brotherly relationship began that very day and it was to last for eleven good years. Not that I knew those things then, but I quickly accepted that Bramble was the top dog... the Alpha... but hey... I was the Beta, and that's no mean thing. I was to be the solid rock that Bramble could always rely on and who always had his back and you know what? I took to that role like a frog to badminton.

# CHAPTER THREE
# HUMANS ARE FUNNY ANIMALS

That year, 2008 really flew past and I crammed so much learning into those months as winter turned to spring... then spring to summer. And suddenly before we knew it autumn began hinting at the cold and dark which was to come with winter's return. Bramble used the time to pass on all his garnered knowledge to me, all his life experience, and as grumpy as Bramble could sometimes be I realized that I now had myself a brother who wouldn't let anything bad happen to me. He taught me the ways of this human world and growled at me often, and many a time told me off when I forgot or ignored his teachings. Bramble was three years older than me... and a lifetime wiser but he went out of his way to let me know that he'd always be there for me... in the good times and the bad.

Mam and dad too became my proper parents... my new forever parents and once I'd realized that they too would always be there for me... I immersed myself in a new, strange and exciting life... a symbiotic relationship between two polar opposite lifeforms who appreciated the foibles and eccentricities of each other. I quickly understood that mam and dad would always feed and look after us, laugh and give us affection for dog antics they didn't remotely understand... and they would protect us. And in return even though we were small we would reciprocate within our limited capabilities to protect them too. The common bond between us was love... given and accepted by both parties in this strange and incredible bonding process. Would I have loved my natural parents more? I don't know... but I think it unlikely... perhaps the same question has been asked many times of human children who have been adopted. No doubt their responses would vary. But my answer will always remain the same... I don't know.

Bramble began his teaching of the human world one day by telling me all he knew and giving examples. We were now into my second or third month. It was a day when we were lying together in our big dog-bed in the living room while mam and dad went shopping in Inverness. Dad had left the back door open and made a sort of enclosure so we could go out for a poo but not too far. Anyhow... Inverness apparently was the big place where all the important people lived. Bramble hadn't seen it himself but he'd heard stories about it being very busy with lots of cars and people and it was near a big deep lake where a famous scary monster lived. That made me worry for a while... in case mam and dad were eaten by the monster... but Bramble said that mam and dad weren't daft and would keep well away from the lake. He began telling me about humans and their lives and it certainly made me think.

*First thing you need to know Bruce is that mam and dad used to be like monkeys.*

*Ehhh... what's a monkey?*

Actually I had a vague idea of what constituted a monkey because I'd seen some on the telly with a human man called David Attenborough the previous evening. Over the following years I came to enjoy watching the telly when animal programmes were on. I'd concluded early on that the television screen thing wasn't just a window that dogs kept disappearing from the side of when they went running off. It was a human thing and I didn't understand it fully but I didn't bark at the telly... even though Bramble did. But I knew Bramble loved showing off his knowledge... hence the monkey question.

*Hmm... well a monkey looks a bit like mam and dad but it's really hairy like us and lives up in trees and eats bendy food called bananas. Monkeys are quite dumb and can't do the chatting thing that mam and dad do and they can only say things like 'ooh-ooh' and make screechy noises.*

*Okay... so when did mam and dad stop being hairy monkeys?*

Bramble had to think about that for a minute, *Dunno for sure but it was definitely before they came for me... so at least four of those year things ago.*

*So where did the hairy bits go to?*

*Ahh... I know that one. They kept the hair on their heads to keep them warm but used one of those razor things to cut all the other hair off.* Dad mustn't have done it the right way because he still needs to scrape hair off his face every day. Mam doesn't so she must have done it properly. *And... because they used to be monkeys that's why they haven't got four legs like us cos their front paws are called hands. They need them for swinging off branches and picking those banana things up.*

That made perfect sense to me even though I'd never seen mam up a tree... so I waited for Bramble to tell me some other human information.

*Next I'm going to tell you how to do staring.*

Staring?

*Aye... it's how you get nice treats.*

That didn't make sense to me, But we get treats.

*Yes but only when mam and dad think we should have one. And they give us those Pedigree twisty things and we don't like them much anyway. You need to learn staring so that they give you chicken and other meaty things off their plates. I've noticed you're not very good at it.*

Okay... so how do you do the staring thing?

*Like this,* said Bramble as he sat up on his haunches and began looking at me in a strange way. His eyes seemed all sad and it made me feel sorry for him but he just kept looking. After a little while he gave me a head grin... lay back down and said, *That's it... that's how you do staring.*

But Bramble that's just looking.

*Bruce... please just learn. When mam and dad are having a meal what do you do? You always go running up to the table and jump up. You start scratching at their legs and that's the wrong thing to do. All that happens is that mam tells you off and makes you go into the dog basket and we don't get any treats. It's spoiling it for me.*

*So...?*

*So walk up slowly and sit beside the table... nice like. Then do that staring thing with sad eyes. If you sit next to me and we've both got sad eyes mam and dad will start to feel guilty about eating their nice food and leaving us out. Then bet you anything you like... a big jumbone or something that dad is the first to give in and drop some chicken or whatever on the floor for us. Then mam will tell him off and then after a while she'll give in too and say something like 'Ohh all right then you two little monkeys,' then she'll cut us some chicken and put it in our bowls. That's what staring can do.*

*Why would mam call us monkeys?*

*Ohhh Bruce... just cos she wants us to be like them... even though we can't.*

*Okay... so then what?*

*Keep doing it when they have their mealtimes and eventually mam will begin to put chicken in our bowls occasionally. When she does make sure you eat up everything in the bowl... even the dog food. Then run around wagging your tail and run up to mam and dad and give them a lick... but only after they've put nice meat in our bowls, not before. That will make them laugh. Then they'll have a good think about things and* before you know it we'll get their nice food lots of times. Mam used to do it for me regularly but she stopped when you came along because you were only allowed puppy food and mam said it wasn't fair. So now we have to train them again.

*Righto Bramble... I've got it. We'll both do it next time that mam does the cooking thing.*

*You're learning Bruce.*

*So are there more things to learn Bramble?*

*A few but I'm tired now.*

*Just one more then Bramble... pretty please.*

He gave me a head frown.

*Promise I won't say any more if you'll just tell me one more thing. Then I'll pipe down and let you have a snooze... please-please-please.*

After a few seconds of huffing and puffing Bramble head-said, *Okay I'm gonna tell you how to find out your long name.*

I didn't have a clue what he was talking about. It had taken me ages just to get used to 'Bruce'. *Ehhh... my human name is Bruce. Even you know that. And your human name is Bramble. What do you mean about my long name?*

Bramble head-grinned, *We've got long names too. It's usually dad who shouts out my long name if I'm being naughty.*

*Ehhh... so what's your long name?*

Bramble's chest seemed to puff out when he looked at me and said...

*Well sometimes it changes but usually it's... Bramble Yool*

*Ittelshit*. He seemed incredibly proud of his full title.

It took me a minute or so to digest that information. I hadn't known anything about long names. So I asked...

*How do I find out my long name? I can't give dad a head-ask because they don't understand dog speak.*

Bramble was in his element imparting knowledge to his little brother. *Next time we take the humans out for playtime, walk really nicely on the lead. Don't pull or anything. Then when we're over the fields and we're free go running off into the gorse bushes and hide. Dad will shout your short name first so that everyone can hear. He'll shout it out about three or four times... but you have to keep hidden. He'll start looking around and poking in the bracken and gorse so make sure you've picked a really good hidey-hole. Then he'll start to get really worried when he can't find out where you are and that's when he'll shout out your long name.*

*Is that it?*

*Yep just do as I say and you'll find out your title.*

I was happy with that and I kept my promise to refrain from asking Bramble any further questions. We snuggled up together and had a nice wee nap until mam and dad returned from the big city. They returned laden with food. Beef and chicken, pork chops and sausages. I reckon dad must have been one of Scotland's mightiest hunters.

It was two days later before I managed to put Bramble's plan into action. Dad was taking us out by himself that day. I walked nicely on the lead all the way to rabbit-land. Then when the lead was taken off I did my usual rolling on my back to give myself a good old scratch. I waited to put our plan into action until dad had thrown the tennis balls for us to chase a few times and we'd had a good sprint around. Then I watched while he turned his back to the wind in order to light one of those puffy white stick things. Now was my moment and I gave Bramble a head wink before running off and hiding in a hollow in the ground behind some trees. I must admit I felt awfully guilty because after a while I could hear that dad was becoming very worried. He was shouting out my short name and his voice was becoming more and more frantic and louder. But you know what?... my brother was right and I found out my full title that day just as Bramble had told me I would.

That day I was really proud because my name was even longer than Bramble's and I became... 'Bruce Flay-Minnell Yerwee-Tossa.'

# CHAPTER FOUR
# HOLIDAY INDEED

The human highlight of 2008 was our four-day trip on a ship to a place they called the Orkneys. The Orkneys turned out to be a lot of little islands to the north of mainland Scotland, and we were to be staying on the biggest of the islands and travelling around 'seeing the sights' as mam and dad put it. We were to be accompanied by mam and dad's friends who had in turn travelled north from a place called Newcastle and were living with us for a few weeks. Their names were John and Jill Sim, and to be honest, I was a little frightened of John at first.

*A policeman is like a postie but more ferocious*, Bramble told me. He explained that policemen had to be good at fighting and chasing naughty people who nicked things. So I kept out of his way for a few days in case he'd heard about the bacon that had fallen out of dad's sandwich and I'd scarpered with it. But pretty soon I came to realise that John was actually a great big softie... and I mean 'really big' because he must have been even taller than a horse... and probably ate more food than two horses.

Jill, however, was little, smaller than mam, and she gave me lots of cuddles and treats. The treats had to be sneaked to me because we weren't supposed to have too many of them as they might make us fat... but somehow Jill always managed to find a way even though I'm sure mam knew what she was doing. And it always seemed that it was mam and Jill who took us for our daily walks on those days before we began the big trip.

Dad and John would stay in the cottage talking about man things... fence posts and rabbit mesh, cars and power tools, politics and motor sport. I quickly learned via Bramble what those words meant and about all the things the men were talking about, but I couldn't understand politics.

*Politics is all about greedy people who like talking and do it as a full-time job,* Bramble explained. *They stand up and tell lies to each other so they can be put in charge of the common human people. Then they stuff their back pockets with paper money that they take from the little people, and they can then afford to live in big houses and make themselves even more important and powerful.*

I gave that information a head swerve because it was way beyond my understanding, and I don't think that Bramble truly fathomed it either. Human behaviour could be very confusing.

I did say that the Orkneys was the highlight of that year. What I actually meant was that it completely turned us two Westies off... but somehow it was enjoyed by the four humans. When we arrived after our long journey, it turned out that Bramble and myself had to be kept on our leads all the time because mam said we were in a strange place and might get lost if we wandered off. I tried to tell the humans that we wouldn't get lost because we could always sniff our way back to them, but I couldn't manage to make them understand. So for those awful Orkney days, we couldn't even have a run around and do play fights or chase rabbits... it was boring.

The humans... mam and dad, Jill and John were very excited however, and they'd made a list of all the things they wanted to see and visit during our stay. The Ring of 'Brodgar' and the Italian Chapel, Skara Brae and finally the Churchill Barriers. Well let me tell you human folk who may be reading this... it was silly and completely and utterly pointless.

The Ring of Brodgar was just a lot of big stones stood up in a circle by some hairy humans from the past who didn't even wear proper clothes and who lived in caves... wow, how great is that? I don't think mam was too impressed either because she didn't bother to tell me off when I had a wee on one of the standing up stones.

Then it was on to the ancient village of Skara Brae. That was where some other really old people had moved out of their caves and made those stone houses instead. But they didn't even have a roof on their houses and their beds were made of flat rocks... and get this folks... they didn't even have duvets. *Must have been some of the first council houses,* Bramble said, but I was none the wiser.

After that there was a visit to the Italian Chapel which

turned out to be an old army shed, but to be fair it did look nice and shiny and clean. However, I still couldn't fathom why anyone would travel all of those miles on a boat to look at an old shed even if it did have nice glittery things inside. *The people who stayed here were called Italians,* Bramble told me, *and they believed that someone called Jesus lived in that shed with his mam.* Hmmm, that sounded fishy to me because we hadn't spotted them. But perhaps they did live there and had just gone out shopping... or there again maybe they'd gone to the pub. Anyway, that's what my brother told me so I reckoned it must be true.

Finally, there was the drive out to see the Churchill Barriers. And big John had become all excited. But guess what? It was just a long road that went over some little islands. *The gaps between the little islands had been filled in with huge rocks so that the Germans who lived under the sea couldn't come into the harbour to sink any more ships,* Bramble explained. He wasn't sure what Germans were but he thought they must be fish. The Germans had sneaked in under the water many years ago and sunk a big aircraft carrier and lots of sailors had been drowned.

The day that we went to see the barriers, Dad and John pulled into a parking place and got out of the car and began pointing and oohing and aahing like schoolboys.

'Look John, look!' cried dad enthusiastically, 'we're looking at Scapa Flow... and over there is where the Royal Oak was sunk,' he said, pointing off into the distance.

'I know... I've always wanted to see this,' replied John

excitedly with a look of satisfaction all over his face. 'I can't believe I'm actually standing here, it's like looking back at history... it's amazing.'

No John, it wasn't... sorry to pee on your trainers and that, but it was just a long stretch of road and a big bay of water and it wasn't anywhere near as big as the sea we used to look at when we were taking walks on the beach at Golspie or Dornoch. Mam and Jill didn't even bother getting out of the car. They were sensible and they munched on sandwiches instead then poured themselves some cups of coffee out of a tartan tube. So why on earth were the men making such a fuss about a not very impressive patch of water? Like I said before, human behaviour could be very confusing.

Then when all sights had been seen and 'oohed' at, we began the long sea journey home the following day. It was extremely unpleasant. The sea was really rough that day and it made us roll all over the place even on the big ship we were travelling on. People were staggering about from side to side as if they were drunk. I didn't enjoy the voyage in the slightest because I kept being sick and Jill kept having to clean up after me. Mam wasn't feeling good either and she was lying on one of the benches below deck. Dad stayed beside mam in case she was sick too.

John however was looking after Bramble out on the top deck. John was up there because he was doing his excited thing again and was really keen to see something he called the 'Old Man of Hoy'... and guess what? It wasn't even a man. It was just a tall skinny rock that stood out amongst the waves all on its lonesome. What on earth was the matter with human folk?... 'ooohh look, a skinny rock sticking up out of the sea, let's use our camera thingy and take some photographs of it.'

My highlight of the day was seeing a pod of dolphins... and they looked so happy and so fast as they skimmed through the choppy water, racing along beside the ship and jumping up in the air and slapping their tails down hard on the water as they landed. I'm sure the lead dolphin kept smiling at me when he leaped in the air, as if to say, 'come and join us little white fella, you'll love it in the sea.' I would have given anything to be a dolphin that day instead of a sad little Westie being ill on a boat. But eventually even the dolphins were left behind and a little while later we docked in a place called Scrabster where we prepared for the return drive to Tain, the cottage and dry land.

Bramble and I were mightily sick of all the travelling at the end of that day, but Jill made sure that we received our reward that same evening. Only one stop had been made on the return journey and that was to buy lots of fish, chips, sausages and haggis from the 'Trawler' chip shop in Golspie. Jill and John bought absolutely loads of food and it smelled delicious even though it made such a stink in the car by the time we reached the cottage.

Mam was still experiencing the after-effects of something called a stroke which she'd been ill with six months before. So with mam still feeling wobbly after the journey, Jill took over in the kitchen and dished out the food for the four exhausted humans. Fish and chips and mushy peas for John, Mam and Jill; haggis, sausage and chips for dad. But sneakily Jill had bought four extra sausages and she contrived to leave them on the floor in the kitchen whilst the two-legged folk congregated around the dining table in the front room. Bramble and I wolfed the sausages down then sneaked back into the sitting room and pretended to be good doggies as we went to our feeding bowls beside the fireplace. Mam couldn't understand why we didn't finish all our proper food that evening but Jill knew the rights of it however and gave us a huge smile when we re-appeared, licking our lips. If I'd known how to do a proper human wink I think I would have sent one across the room to Jill... she was being a very nice but naughty human.

\* \* \* \* \*

Then life moved on and Jill and John returned to their home in Newcastle and we carried on with our fabulous lives out there in the Ross-shire countryside. Every day offered up something different and it was such an exciting time to be a Westie.

Dad was putting up new fences and rabbit mesh to fence in the new land he had bought and to keep those hairy little fellas out of his vegetable garden. Mam seemed to never be away from her polytunnel and neighbours would keep appearing to be given a basket of tomatoes, a bag of peppers or a cucumber. I soon learned who the good neighbours were and they were always nice and friendly with Bramble and myself... some of them even sneaked biscuits to us when mam wasn't watching.

One of the treat-sneakers was a lady called Sandra who lived in a house down the track and a little distance away from us over the main road. She would let dad have horse manure in return for her bagful of vegetables and she often came past our cottage riding one of her horses and guess what... I wasn't frightened of Sandra's horses even though they were really big.

I spent many hours out in the huge garden with dad too and would watch with interest as he worked long hours digging potatoes, plucking strawberries, picking sprouts from their tough stalks and filling the kitchen with swedes, cabbage, parsnips and carrots. I would trot along dutifully with Bramble as dad designed a new flower garden area for mam and he erected lots of trelliswork for the climbing plants that mam loved, especially the ones she called honeysuckle and clematis. Our cottage garden became a focal point for the neighbours to gather and for visitors to come and stay with us and admire the transformation mam and dad had made.

For their own particular reasons the human highlight of the year had been our trip with Jill and John to the Orkneys, but for myself and Bramble the highlight was Christmas day. For myself this was to be the first of many Christmas celebrations and my brother spent a lot of time telling me about what to expect and to prepare me for the big event that humans loved so much. I was a little sceptical about Bramble's enthusiastic description of the big day to come... but I was to be completely surprised.

One cold day, leaving dad in the house, we set off for a walk down the track with mam to play with our friend Cuillin. He was a big springer spaniel who some nice people called Jim and Wendy had rescued from the island of Skye, hence the name and he was a big friendly lump so we used to go down to his house quite regularly for a game of chasey or football. He was much faster than Bramble and myself and always got to the ball first but we still had a great time just running around. Even though Cuillin was much bigger than us he was very wary of Bramble who would warn him off when he began being too rough with me. Bramble would face him and give a low throaty growl and Cuillin would back away. I realised at that point that my brother was the real deal and would do anything to protect me.

Bramble said that John used to be a policeman but I didn't know what that meant. So, on that day in particular we seemed to be out for much longer than usual and the reason for that would be obvious when we returned home.

I was first through the back door that day and headed straight for the sitting room. Bramble had been lagging behind with mam but came shooting into the room like a streak of lightning when he heard my furious barking.

*Bruce... what's wrong?* he head shouted. Then he saw me barking frantically at the corner of the room behind the settee.

*Quick Bramble... quick. There's a bloody huge tree growing out of the floor and it's covered in shiny string and round things. It must have grown up really quickly while we were out* at Cuillin's house. Woof-woof-woof.

Calm yourself down Bruce, it's okay. Stop your barking, it's mam and dad's Christmas tree... like I was telling you. Dad's been putting it up while we were out of the house.

That's daft Bramble, you can't grow trees in your house, they're meant to be outside for birds to sit in.

It's not a proper tree Bruce. It's a pretend tree that mam and dad put there every year in the winter.

It looks real to me, I head-said... still giving the tree the evil eye and growling at it. There was even a little girl in a white dress sitting on top of the tree like a bird. I didn't like this turn of events one little bit but Bramble was adamant that this was all perfectly normal and just another example of daft human behaviour. So I calmed down but I still kept my eye on the monstrosity just in case... if that big tree so much as moved on its own I'd be over there to give it a good old bite on the trunk.

Then over the following week boxes wrapped in shiny paper and decorated with bows began to accumulate beneath the tree. I couldn't wait to get at that shiny stuff but Bramble had warned me off and told me in no uncertain terms, *Bruce you haven't got to touch those things under the tree. They're called presents and mam and dad give them to each other when an old fat man squeezes down the chimney and comes out of the fireplace on a day that they call Christmas. I've never seen him because he comes at night but mam and dad leave some pies and some beer out for him so they must know who he is.*

*Aye, but Bramble we can hear better than mam and dad. If a fat old man is coming out of the fireplace he must make a noise. You must have heard him surely?*

*I know Bruce, you would think so wouldn't you? But I've had three of these Christmases now and this one will be number four and in all that time I've not heard him even once. The really strange thing is that he doesn't even leave any scent behind. I've sniffed and sniffed but I still don't know what that old man they call Santa Claus smells like.*

I wasn't happy with that.. no way. *Bramble that's daft anyway because if he's a fat man like you say then he couldn't come down the chimney. Even a skinny man couldn't come down there and even if he could he'd be all dirty and black when he came out and would leave a mess all over and if the fire was on he would burn himself. Maybe he doesn't really come. Maybe mam and dad just think that a fat old man has come down the chimney.*

*Bruce... mam and dad aren't stupid. They get up in the morning of the Christmas Day thing and you can hear them being excited and saying things like 'Ooohh Jim look Santa's left lots of presents for us... and he's left some presents for Bramble too'... And I don't know why he doesn't leave any smell behind Bruce. Mam and dad think he's like something called magic. Maybe those magic humans don't have any smell.*

*That's daft Bramble, everything has a smell.*

*I know that. But I can't explain why he hasn't. It must be some strange human stuff that we don't understand but you'll* believe it about Santa when mam and dad show you the presents he's left for you and then let you tear the paper off.

Presents for me. Like what?

I don't know what he'll give you... maybe some balls and some toys and meaty strip things. You might even get a tartan jacket like mine.

I'd laughed the first time I'd seen Bramble in his tartan jacket but now I was quite jealous when we went for a walk and Bramble was wearing it. If what Bramble said was true then I was now looking forward to the old man coming out of our fireplace and leaving me a box wrapped in shiny paper with a spanking new tartan jacket all of my own. Roll on Christmas and roll on fat man... but please don't get stuck up the flue. Now I was excited.

Christmas Day turned out to be all that Bramble had said... and more. Because mam and dad were excited it rubbed off on me and I was excited too. Then mam put a pile of presents in front of Bramble and myself... six each, and finally gave us the signal to begin. We tore into those boxes and parcels like Rottweilers. It was super fun and me and Bramble were head laughing with each other as we destroyed the paper and the cardboard boxes. There were biscuits and treats in packets, squeaky balls and squeaky toys. One of my squeaky toys looked just like a fox and I tried desperately to shake the squeak out of him but I had to give up when I became too tired. It was to take me many weeks before I shut the bugger up. That old fox kept squeaking away for ages. Among the presents there was a proper football too which Bramble told me we'd have to share with dad because he enjoyed playing on the lawn in the back garden as well. But my big present was as I'd hoped... a tartan jacket exactly the same as the one Bramble wore... only mine was blue tartan instead of red. I couldn't wait for our next walk and I was hoping that the weather would stay cold so that I could wear it.

Now, I realise that some of you sensible people who are reading this may laugh... and I don't blame you because it sounds daft, but that was the day I began to believe in the magic human called Santa Claus and you know what... I didn't care a less whether the old fat guy left a smell behind or not.

# CHAPTER FIVE
# A PLACE CALLED ROGART

I was four years old and a few months short of my fifth birthday when we moved out of our cottage at Northwilds and into our new home in Pittentrail in the parish of Rogart in Sutherland. I was sad to leave our old home and all our lovely neighbours, but mam and dad were getting older and the land we had was taking a lot of looking after, so they'd bought a house with a smaller garden. They'd also had altercations with some unfriendly neighbours and dad couldn't be bothered to fight with the man that everyone, even the police, called the fantasist, so we relocated. The village we moved to was also good for mam and dad because our new house stood close to the local Spar shop and the local pub called the Pittentrail Inn. Dad was really enthusiastic about that... mam not so much.

It took Bramble and I a few weeks to introduce ourselves to all the neighbours in the village, but we enjoyed the process and we didn't meet a single human who wasn't friendly... well only one. The people talked quite funnily though... not the same as mam and dad and sometimes they were hard to understand. But as we weren't supposed to be able to understand human talk anyway, it didn't make much difference to us Westies.

Bramble and I lay together one evening in the big dog bed that mam and dad had bought us for our new sitting room. We proceeded to have another of our long head chats and probably the longest talk that we'd ever had.

The new village had thrown up so many questions and there was so much new stuff to get our heads around. There were a number of things I'd found difficult to fathom, so I began.

'Bramble... what does boobs mean?'

'Boobs?'

'Aye... boobs. I heard Jean from next door talking with mam about a woman in the village but mam didn't know who she meant... so Jean said "It's the blonde woman who drives the Land Rover... you'll know who I mean she's got massive boobs". So I was just wondering what boobs are. Are they big dogs or something?'

Bramble gave a laugh. 'Aahh... I know what they are. They're the chest things that women humans have. Men humans don't have them and they have flat chests but women humans have two bags on their chests for feeding their puppies. Can you remember your dog mam? She had those bags underneath for feeding her puppies too with milk.'

That made me think. 'So *why have humans only got two bags? Dog mam had lots for feeding all my brothers and sisters. What happens when the human mams' have three or four puppies. Who gets to drink the milk and who gets left out?*'

Bramble was deep in thought.

'*What do the human puppies that haven't got a bag to feed from do? What do they eat?*'

Bramble gave a head grin, '*Cheese toasties and Cornettos.*'

'*Ehhh... what's that?*'

'*Baby food for the ones left out.*'

'*Really?*'

'*Aye of course... I've heard the humans talking about it.*'

I wasn't sure if Bramble had just made that up but I decided it was probably true. Anyway that was my question answered but I had plenty more.

'*What are you going to do about that fox up the meadow Bramble?*' At the back of our house was a huge meadow, leading on to trees and hills and streams and I'd spotted a big fox on a few occasions and he would just sit there watching us from a distance.

'Nothing,' he answered.

That was strange, '*Why not? I've seen him twice now.*'

'Cos he's a big bugger Bruce and foxes aren't softies.'

'Aye Bramble but he won't be as tough as you.'

'Don't kid yourself Bruce... I might be tough but that fox isn't just going to let me win if we have a fight. He might run away but that's not because he's scared. It's because he has more sense than to fight all the dogs he sees. He's independent and lives out in the countryside even in winter so that makes him extra tough. Anyway he hasn't done us any harm. He hasn't done anyone any harm apart from the rabbits.'

'Aye but I heard that lady from over the dip say that the fox had killed some of her hens. That's not right is it?'

'No it's not but it's not my problem. That woman should send one of her tough hens to fight the fox.'

'That's daft Bramble... hens can't fight.'

'No... fair enough but cocks can. They're the big stroppy ones with the comb thing on their heads. You don't want to mess with one of those fellas. They're tough cookies and if you get too close they'll peck your eyes out or give you a nasty cut with their spurs. Don't think for a moment that they're just like hens, because they're not.'

Hmmm... that was news to me but the one thing I had learned in my four years of being with Bramble was never to doubt him. He knew lots of things and of course he was always there to protect me. I had lots of questions on my mind though.

'You know that little lad down the street who keeps coming past the garden and saying hello. What were you showing him the other day?'

'Nothing... I don't know what you mean.'

'Aye you do Bramble I saw you on the football field. He was kicking a ball around and you were chasing it, then afterwards you started showing him something.'

Bramble gave a think grin, 'Ohhh aye that. He's not that young. He's about twelve or something. Anyway I couldn't get inside the lad's head. It's a shame because he's alright but I couldn't get through to him.'

'So what were you trying to teach him?'

'Ha-ha-ha,' Bramble had a long chuckle to himself. 'I was trying to show him the proper way to go to bed... you know? How to scrunch the blankets up and turn around three or four times before lying down. But he didn't understand... it's a pity.'

'He won't be coming back then?'

'Ohhh yes he will. He's a smart lad and we get on well together. I'm going to try and teach him how to lick his bum next.'

I wasn't so sure about that, 'Do you think he'll be bendy enough Bramble?'

Bramble thought hard about that for a while... then, 'Dunno really... but I'll give it a try. Anyhow it would be much better than having to ask one of his friends to lick his bum.'

'Aye there's that I suppose.'

'Anyway Bruce it's time we were getting some shuteye.' Bramble snuggled himself down with his backside pushed into my tummy. I put a leg over his shoulder.

'Just one more question Bramble.'

'Aahh Bruce I'm really tired. What do you want now?'

'What did that woman mean when she was shouting at mam last week? The woman with that huge dog that she couldn't control?'

'I don't know Bruce. I didn't hear it. It must have been the day that I stayed in the house because of the paw mites that were driving me crazy.'

'Ohhh aye... it was that day. Is it all better now? If I remember the dog doctor gave you some cat-worming tablets to see if they would help.'

'Aye Bruce they worked. Those mites were making me want to bite my paws off. They're nasty little buggers.'

'Ha-ha-ha... cat worming tablets. That means you're a right pussy.'

'Are you wanting a good bashing or something Bruce? If you tell any of the other village dogs about the cat tablets you'll be in for it. Call me a pussy again if you dare.'

I didn't dare. But I still wanted to know what that rude woman with the crazy dog had shouted at mam. I waited a few seconds to let Bramble calm down.

'So mam told the woman that she shouldn't be out in the village with a ferocious dog that didn't have a muzzle on. She'd let it out of a big caravan thing that pulled up outside the pub and as soon as it saw me and mam it was trying to get at us and bite us. That's when mam told the woman off but she just laughed and said, "Awa and bile yer heid" so what *does that mean Bramble?'*

Bramble knew immediately... he usually did. 'It means she was a rude woman from a place called Glasgow and what she shouted at mam meant for her to go and boil her head.'

'Ehhh?'

'It's what people from that place say when they're being rude and nasty.'

'But that's really silly cos how could mam boil her own head? She'd need a really big pan and she'd have to take her head off to put it in the boiling water but if she did that then her eyes would be in the pan so she wouldn't be able to see what she was doing with just a neck and no head.'

'Good night Bruce.'

'What?'

'Go to sleep and stop jabbering on... I'm tired.'

'But what about mam's head?'

'Goodnight Bruce.'

'Much help you are Bramble... good night. Will you explain tomorrow?'

'Yes.'

'Good night again.'

'Shut it Bruce.'

I did.

\*\*\*\*\*

Life was brilliant for we two Westies for the remainder of the year and we had great fun making friends with all of our next-door neighbour's spaniels. Jean was the lady in the village who fostered and rehomed spaniels who for one reason or another had fallen on hard times. Maybe their human parents had fallen on hard times themselves and couldn't keep them or maybe they'd even died. Sometimes it was because people had been cruel to the spaniels and made them frightened and unhappy. Jean had four spaniels of her own and quite often she looked after her daughter's two dogs so there was always fun and games going on.

Bramble and I looked forward to our trips to the meadow when Jean was there with the spaniels and we would run around together having a real good time. The spaniels were much faster than Bramble and I… all apart from Liath I think, who was the oldest of them but she was really nice and just walked along slowly.

Jean and mam would talk quite often over the back fence and Jean would give mam loads of advice about dog behaviour. Some of it sounded really sensible and she obviously knew what she was talking about. One day I heard them talking.

'Ohhh Jean I've been trying for ages to make that special connection with Bruce… to make him understand and make him think more like a human. But it's not working. What do you think I should do?'

'Nothing Lorraine… you're approaching the problem from the wrong direction. You'll never get to understand any of your Westies if you try and make them think like a human. Reverse that thought and begin thinking like a Westie... you'll find the problem stops being a problem and both you and Bruce will have a brilliant relationship. Remember that your dogs are just children with fur coats.'

'Yeh but Jean... dogs don't speak.'

'Oh yes they do Lorraine... but only to those who know how to listen.'

Mam thought about that statement for a while then said, 'So how do I know when they're in a good mood? They can't laugh and tell me when I'm doing things right and let me know how happy they are.'

'Of course they can Lorraine. They do laugh but they laugh with their tails.'

That advice from Jean really turned my relationship with mam and dad on its head and pretty soon we were cosying along with a mutual respect and understanding. Bramble too benefited from Jean's advice and the difference it made to our household was profound. We were no longer in a master and dogs relationship... we were in an alliance of equals. Even so mam and dad still had to pick up our poo... ha-ha.

# CHAPTER SIX
# BRAMBLE LIFE-GUARD

My brother Bramble was beginning to slow down and it was sad. We were into the year that the humans called 2015 and Bramble was turning ten years old. Certainly not a huge age for us Westies, but he'd been through such a lot with various health complaints. He'd had to have an operation on his cruciate and now he found it difficult to climb the stairs. He found it embarrassing to be carried up and down the stairs at bedtime and in the morning. He'd had terrible trouble with paw mites for a long time and the vets had tried various remedies, but none with great success until one of the junior vets called Clare had pulled mam to one side and suggested that she try a Milbemax cat worming tablet on Bramble. Within a week of beginning his cat regime, Bramble's paws cleared up completely, and although he had to take those tablets regularly, the paw mites never returned. There were various other ailments like dermatitis and grass seeds in the ear canal, but my brother Bramble just soldiered on and got on with living.

That was until the day of the attack by a big out-of-control dog who had set his sights on me and marked me down as his next victim. Bramble saved me that day with no thoughts of his own safety. He was alpha male and he did his job. My brother saved my life that day and almost lost his own, but he never once referred to the attack again. He did what was expected of him... in his own mind, and I'll always be thankful that he had accepted me as his brother. Unfortunately, he was never the same after that, but I still played the second fiddle role. It never crossed my mind to be lead dog. I wasn't up for it and couldn't handle the responsibility, and I never once let Bramble think that he was anything but the boss.

The attack that day was vicious. An out-of-control dog with an out-of-control owner who had no idea of how to handle a canine. Why little humans have to have huge dogs I'll never understand.

We'd had a lovely walk that morning alongside the river Fleet with mam, and we'd even chased a few rabbits. Not mam, of course, because she never chased rabbits, and anyway she was quite old now and nowhere near as fast as a Westie. So we were walking through the village... both on our leads in case a car or lorry came past, and mam was singing away to herself... something called 'One Day at a Time', and Bramble and me were trying to close our ears off because mam sounded like a cat with bronchitis. Then it happened.

A huge roar that sounded more like a tiger than a dog. I looked around quickly and there was a huge ferocious beast heading straight for me. He looked like a hound from hell as he leapt at me, and I couldn't run away because I was still on my lead. Then Bramble leapt at the dog and pushed the monster away from me. Bramble wasn't even a third of the size of the attacker, and that big bugger was going wild and was completely out of control.

Bramble was bitten and bleeding that day. The big dog had Bramble in his mouth, shaking him like a rag-doll until a woman ran out of the house and began bashing the big dog until he dropped Bramble. I was in shock but I was ready to fight if that thing came back for a second attack. I let out a series of brave barks and head-shouted at the big dog... 'You're in for it now because we have some big tough friends... you're round the twist you menace.'

To cut a long story short and bypassing some of the more gruesome details, mam took me home to stay with dad while she drove Bramble to the vets'. It would be two days before we got to know if my brother was to live or die. The vet was concerned that Bramble's internal organs may be seriously damaged, and for the next few days mam and dad were very subdued. It would be a week or more before my brother was allowed home, and when we were reunited, Bramble too was subdued and a lot quieter. He spent the next two weeks with a dog-hood to stop him from licking his wounds, which were many and angry. And as I said before, he was never the same after that attack. He still head-talked like the old Bramble but he seemed to have lost a lot of confidence, and I felt so sorry for my big brother.

***Bramble and Bruce – Me at the front (for once)***

    The police and the SPCA came to the house soon after the attack, and they asked mam if she wanted the attack dog to be put down. Mam said no because she wouldn't be able to live with that on her conscience, but she did ask the man from the SPCA if he could put the owner down instead. He said no... then smiled at mam and dad and said he wished he could.

✳ ✳ ✳ ✳

So life moved on and Bramble recovered. During the next few years we even made friends with a standard Poodle. That took a while to be fair because when we first saw 'Marmaduke' we couldn't believe our eyes. He had big puff-ball bits of hair on his head, his knees, ankles and also his tail. He looked like a real poser. At first Bramble and myself thought he must be a member of some weird religious cult but not so. He was actually quite friendly and quite annoyed that his daft mam made him go and prance around at things called dog-shows when all he really wanted to do was roll around on the grass and chase balls. Marmaduke was nice... his mam was nuts.

For the next few years we would have many days on the beach together, Bramble and I. Dornoch and Golspie were our favourites, but we also had many days in Tain on the riverside walk and a lot of days climbing the local hills. We still chased rabbits on our hill days but I knew better than to catch one if mam was watching. Sometimes I'd catch up with one of the baby rabbits but I'd always just have a sniff and leave the little bundle of fluff alone because they would be terrified.

Then came the day that I'd been dreading. My last day with my brother Bramble.

I'd known for a few weeks that he was deteriorating. Sometimes he would just fall over to the side, and even though he quickly recovered, it was noticeable that he was just running out of energy. On that final day we went for a walk up to the meadow. I walked along beside my brother but he was so slow and his head-talk with me didn't make much sense. I remember he said something like *'I'm going to be with dog-mam soon Bruce... and I'm really looking forward to it. I hope she still remembers me.'*

I didn't know what to say... so I kept quiet. Then after a little trot around Bramble lay down in the grass and he was panting. All energy was gone and dad knelt down, gave him a stroke then carefully picked him up. We began the walk back home. Dad had tears in his eyes but Bramble seemed to be at peace with the world in dad's arms.

*'It's been a pleasure to have known you Bruce. I'm proud to call you my brother and my best friend. Take care of mam and dad and don't be sad.'*

Mam was waiting at the front door. She looked at dad then down at the floor.

'Is it time?'

'Aye... it's time.'

Mam bent her head down to give Bramble a kiss. He gave a little moan and licked mam's cheek then he licked her tears as she began to cry. *'Don't cry mam,'* he head-said, *'it's my time to move on and that's a good thing. Tell her it's okay Bruce and look after her because she's going to be so sad.'*

Then my brother was gone. He went off in the car with mam and dad but he never came home. Mam and dad returned but the house was strangely quiet and they talked in whispers about something called a brain tumour. I was so distraught... my brother had left this life and he'd left me too... all on my lonesome, except for mam and dad of course. I'm sure he would have stayed if he could... but I know he would have been unhappy to live on in ill health. God bless Bramble... you're with your dog family now... please save a place for me and speak well of me. I love you... you grumpy old bugger.

## CHAPTER SEVEN
## JACK IN THE BOX

The next month was hard for mam and dad but even more so for me. All the places I used to go with Bramble I was now mooching around on my own. Golspie in particular was really difficult because it had been Bramble's favourite place along the golf-course track, and even though mam and dad were trying to be kind, I'd still have a whiff of Bramble in the areas he regularly left his scent. I was missing my big brother and I kept finding traces of him in the weirdest of places. I realised early on that I didn't have any enthusiasm without my best pal. I was now part of a one-dog family and I didn't like it... because something important was missing.

Then one day whilst out on our Golspie walk, we bumped into the dog lady who rescued all manner of abused and lonely dogs. She always had five or six dogs walking with her. Two of them were always muzzled because they'd been so badly used during their lives that they were frightened of people and would attack if given the chance as a first line of defence. They'd been used as something called 'bait dogs' by lunatic humans who cared nothing for animals' lives and who would take pleasure from watching dogs tear each other to bits. Robbie, however, was different. An easy-going cross of uncertain parentage but as friendly as you like. My mam and his mam were having a good old talk one day when he wandered across... then gave me a good sniff and said...

'What's up with you? You look down in the dumps.'

'What's that got to do with you?'

'Nowt... nae problem Bruce... forget I asked.' He turned to go.

'Sorry Robbie, I'm being awfully rude.'

'So what's up?'

'My brother's just gone and died.'

'Aye... so what?'

'He was my brother.'

'Aye... and?'

'He's gone... away to dog heaven mam says. But it's just not fair. He isn't here for me anymore.'

'So what's with the long face?'

It took me a while to respond but then I said, 'He was the leader... my brother and I don't know how to go on without him.'

'I've lost four or five.'

'What?'

'Brothers... sisters... friends, you lose them all the time. That's what happens. All things come to an end... dog, human... everything. Nothing lasts forever.'

'So what do you do?'

'Accept that life also means end of life. If you've had a good life with your humans then rejoice because so many of us never have that chance of happiness. Ask your humans for a new companion.'

'But it won't be Bramble my brother.'

'No... it will be another who you'll learn to love too. We're all on the same journey. I'll be gone myself soon Bruce and I reckon you won't be long after. Fourteen seems to be about the number when we all find our peace. Let another someone into your life and give that new pal all the love that your Bramble gave to you. He was a grouchy old git wasn't he?... but he protected you and looked after his humans. Time for you to step up to the plate... as they say. You'll never forget him but you'll learn to cope without him. Let your mam and dad know how lonely you are and before you know it you'll have a different pal to share with.' With that final comment he turned and trotted away... and those head-words gave me food for thought.

\* \* \* \* \*

I don't know how I managed to show mam and dad how depressed I was without my brother and best mate. Probably they'd noticed that I wasn't interested in my food apart from the few mouthfuls I would take even when my bowl had nice chicken or beef in it. I was sleeping a lot and my walks had become less enjoyable. There wasn't a best pal to turn to and to whom I could say, *'here, have a sniff at this... must have been a badger out last night,'* life was empty without Bramble. However, after a few weeks had passed I noticed mam and dad were talking in whispers and making secret phone calls. I was eleven years old and feeling sad and lonely but I was also ready for a new adventure.

Adventure would be the operative word because I was totally unprepared for the dynamic ball of fluff and illness that was to invade my life that weekend.

Dad had set off early on the Saturday morning with Uncle Jack driving the car and both accompanied by a nice Polish lady called Kasia whom dad had been teaching English. They were heading for a place called Lockerbie which was a long way away from our home in Sutherland. I had the weirdest feeling that I was going to be surprised that day... and boy-oh-boy what a surprise it would turn out to be.

That day dragged by so slowly and for most of it I lay on the couch with my head on mam's lap. We'd been for our walk of course but only as far as the local football field and there hadn't been any other local dogs about for a run around or a head-talk. I had a good feed that day because mam was giving off excitement vibes and every half-hour or so she'd go to the front window, part the blinds and look out for dad's car. We were a week or so into the month that the humans called October and the dark evenings were upon us now.

Then dad returned and my new brother made his first

appearance.

He was nothing more than a little bundle of white fluff and it only took one of dad's hands to carry him as he came in through the front door.

***Wee Jack's First Photo***

I said one of dad's hands but to be honest after a few months he became much more than just a handful. The poor little mite who was to take up the mantle of new little brother was in such ill health that I didn't know how long he would be with us. He was desperately ill and mam and dad were so worried about him that I took something of a back seat for quite a while. I wasn't bothered because I was used to being number two dog and that position suited me perfectly... but I was worried for my new-found relative whom mam and dad had named Jack. Dad had wanted to call him Nobby after some footballer and also after his first dog but mam put her foot down and said no. It didn't really matter because whatever the little fella's name he deserved better than illness.

He seemed fine that first day and all through the following weeks and he did all the puppy things that I remembered doing. Weeing on the carpet... jumping all over the place... pestering me for play fights, chewing slippers and puppy-biting hands. He even ate lots of the special puppy food that mam and dad had bought and everything seemed as it should be.

It must have been the second or third month that he began to exhibit some awful signs. He began to vomit after eating and when he poo'd it was just a load of slimy black squelch and blood. Mam and dad didn't take him to the dog doctor immediately because they thought it may just have been a reaction to the puppy injections he'd recently had.

It wasn't a reaction though because my poor little brother was diagnosed with something called chronic colitis. The next twelve months were horrid and Jack seemed to never be away from the vet. He looked so emaciated... skinny and sad. But during his little spells of decent health he was funny and intelligent and it was during those periods that we would have our head-talks.

I took it upon myself to impart all the knowledge that my departed brother Bramble had given to me. Jack soaked it up like a sponge and fairly quickly I concluded that my new brother... although regularly poorly, was much smarter than me. He was so quick on the uptake that sometimes it was actually scary to realise how clever he was. He would watch the television like a little human and at times he would try to speak... and to be honest he sounded almost human. I often wondered what Bramble would have made of him because Jack had been born just two days after Bramble left us. I sometimes thought that maybe he'd managed to make his way back to me in the form of a puppy. Life was certainly strange during that period.

\*\*\*\*\*

We were well into Jack's third year when I began to feel very poorly. Jack's colitis had improved because of something called research that dad had been doing. Jack's colitis episodes were now about twelve days apart and he looked much better. He'd put on weight and his fur now looked nice and shiny and his episodes had shrunk in their intensity. My little brother was being a brave little trooper and a super friend. I felt blessed.

It was during one of our head-talks one day that Jack looked at me strangely and came right out with... *'You're not very well are you Bruce?'*

I didn't want to lie to my little brother but I purposely neglected to tell him that I'd overheard Neil the vet telling mam and dad that my kidneys were packing in. I'd deduced from that it would soon be my turn to leave this world to be with Bramble and my dog relations. I was thirteen years old but it seemed like fourteen was maybe out of the question.

'No Jack I'm not. I'm feeling old and tired and there's something wrong inside my tummy.'

'Yeah Bruce... but mam and dad and the dog doctor will make you feel better won't they?'

I didn't reply.

'They will though... won't they Bruce?'

'We'll see Jack... we'll see.'

I left it for a number of weeks before I finally told little Jack that I would need to leave him soon. Because he'd been through such a lousy time himself I didn't want to upset him but he didn't seem surprised.

'I know Bruce... I've known for a while. I've heard mam and dad talking and I can see that you're not yourself. At first Iwas really sad but now I'm not so upset because I know that we all have to find our way back to our dog families sometime. You're going to see your best friend Bramble. I know you still love him because you talk about him all the time and tell me how brave he was. Then you'll be able to see your dog mam and all the brothers and sisters you've told me about too... all the "Sniff" family.'

That was the day I began to feel comfortable about my

last weeks. I did still worry about mam and dad but I knew in my own mind that Jack was grown-up enough now to take care of them. My life had been full of love from my human family and I'd been blessed with two great brothers so now was not the time for sadness and regret but a time to rejoice for a life well lived.

# CHAPTER EIGHT
# GOODBYE FOLKS

So my story ends more or less as it began as I lie here in the arms of my human mam. Dad has promised that he'll tell my story to the world so that I'm never forgotten. That makes me so proud. I'm really desperately tired now and I can't stand up without help. Dad is putting Jack's tartan collar on to take him for a solo walk up on the top field while mam and myself wait for the nice vet man to come and help me along with the return journey to reunite with my dog family. I've already said my goodbyes to my little brother but even so he jumps up onto the couch and gives me a final kiss.

'Bye Bruce.'

'Bye Jack.'

'Please tell your Bramble that you found a nice little brother when he moved on... and ask him to be nice to me when it's my time.'

'I will Jack... I promise. You and Bramble will get on great anyway. You're a gutsy little fella. Take care of those two hu-

*mans and tell the other village dogs all about me please... how brave I was.'*

'I will Bruce.'

Then the front door bell rings and I can hear little Jack and dad crying as they're leaving the house and the nice vet man comes into the sitting room. Mam cuddles me in and kisses me. I can feel her tears on my face... but I feel strangely at peace as the vet man opens his bag.

Goodbye human world... it's been a privilege and a blast. Bye mam... bye dad you were the best.

# WEE JACK'S POSTSCRIPT (BY HIS DAD)

Jack did miss his brother terribly for a number of weeks. Fortunately, another family moved into the village very close to us. A nice couple called Michael and Lesley with two teenage kids... Aidan and Teagan. Luckily for us they also had a Springer Spaniel pup called Torin. Jack and Torin met up and after some initial growling they became firm friends... which deflected some of the pain Jack was feeling over the loss of his brother Bruce. Jack's colitis... whilst not cured has improved dramatically and the flare-ups have decreased to such an extent that we're now looking at maybe a few months between very mild episodes. We sourced Jack's health regime ourselves because our local vet practice seemed unable to give the kind of improvement we hoped for other than offer expensive bags of kibble which we don't even feed him anymore. Long may the improvement continue.

But this isn't Jack's story... or indeed Bruce or Bramble's story. It's the tale of three individual Westies with diverse traits and personalities who have in their own inimitable ways enriched our human lives tremendously. We take our hats off to our three hairy kids... Bramble, Bruce and Jack, and we hope all three are waiting for us when it's our turn to depart this life and move over. So that's it folks... the end.

# THE END
## 'AS IF'

Aye... end indeed. How on earth did mam and dad think they'd let a book go to print without my input?

Wee Jack here... but not so wee anymore. I'm four now. Why flying insects have knees I don't know but I'm convinced I'm in possession of those ones belonging to bees. I've heard mam and dad say that I'm the bees-knees.

Let me tell you folks who are reading my offering a little bit about myself. I know this whole tale was written by Bruce and it is essentially his story (helped by dad of course with the spelling). But I can't let my brother's passing go by without me having my say. He was the best brother of all time. I didn't ever meet Bramble who was gone a wee while before my entrance but I do know that Bruce felt the same way about his big brother as I felt about my big brother. Brucie was calm and quiet and he enjoyed his position as number two dog. He hated taking the lead and as soon as I stopped being a mad pup he let me take the Alpha role. That made him feel comfortable and we slipped into our relationship so easily that it just seemed the natural way of things.

The next photograph is one of the times Brucie and I shared together both splayed out on the settee. It's my favourite.

***Bruce and Jack – Sleepy Brothers***

# BRUCE AND JACK
# SLEEPY BROTHERS

That's me at the bottom of the photo and Brucie on the duvet. He had a bit of arthritis by then so I let him have the comfortable bed. Sorry about showing my bits but we Westies aren't shy.

Life without Bruce was desperately unhappy. I missed him so much... I still do in fact. I don't think there's ever a day goes by that I don't think of him. It's not as if he was ever in command or anything but he was always there by my side. I was the big skyscraper but he was my solid foundation. I was the star but he was my spaceship. I was the Roman Candle but he was the match that lit me up. You don't see dogs cry because we do it with our tails... and mine stopped wagging. I missed him then and to be honest I still miss him now. Love you Bruce... and by extension Bramble.

Fortunately for myself it was no more than a few weeks after Bruce left us that I first set eyes on Torin. He was a daft Springer Spaniel pup and he was out on the football field for a walk with his human mam. I was three years old by then and quite mature so it came as something of a shock when this daft Springer pup rushed over the field and began jumping all over me. I gave him a good old growl and warned him off... but it didn't stop him. He didn't have the cut-off button that comes with maturity and he came back for more. We ended up having a growly fight and I had to give him a nip before sensibility kicked in and he backed off. He did the lying on his back surrender thing and I gave him a head talk.

*'You need to get your dopey head sorted out quickly or you'll end up getting a right good bash-and-bite from one of the big dogs.'*

*'Ehhh... who said that? where's that voice coming from?'* he jumped up from his prone position and began turning circles... frantically trying to find the source of the voice.

*'We're head talking you dummy.'*

*'Ehhh... what's that?'*

It took me a little while to explain head-talking to him as we trotted around the field... because Springers are really dumb until they're about three or four years old. Eventually he got the hang of sending and receiving but it didn't make him more sensible. Even now over a year later he's still as daft as a brush (don't ask why humans say brushes are daft because I don't know) but it's definitely something they say. Maybe some of the brushes are quite intelligent... because I know mam's got one she's named Bex-Bissell but it's never said a word to me... it's a mystery.

✳ ✳ ✳ ✳ ✳

So now that my friendship problem was sorted out it came the time that my chronic colitis was next on the agenda. I'd had quite a rubbish time of it with vomiting and black slimy poos from about my fourth month onwards... and my stomach would be squeaking and growling. It wasn't good for mam and dad either as they would be out with me sometimes during the night because I felt so poorly. I'd feel like rubbish for a day... sometimes two days and then I'd be okay for five or six days before it began all over again. Mam seemed to constantly have me at the vets and dad wasn't happy with the vet people because they always seemed to just want to sell dad big bags of expensive kibble. Dad said it was because the Americans were taking over the local vet practices and all they cared about was money. So it was then that dad began his own research.

It was only a few months before Bruce left us that mam and dad changed our food. Bruce hadn't been eating much for a while but the new food enthused even him. No more kibble for we Westies. It was good to see my brother enjoying his grub and I loved it too. Dad would keep a record of my colitis episodes and before long they only came every two weeks... but then Bruce left us to join his dog mam and dad and his real brothers and sisters. For a few weeks it was all we could do just to keep going and pretending that life was normal. It wasn't of course because our family had always been like a rowing boat and for weeks after Bruce left us there was a big gaping hole in it: but somehow we all kept bailing.

Then as the weeks rolled by there came the day when a package arrived for dad. It was a tub... delivered by a man called Amazon and it had an interesting aroma. Mam and dad talked about it; then gave it a shake and a sniff before reading through the instructions and guidance. Next day after my morning meal I followed mam through to the kitchen for my usual 'Turkey Tender' treat... and beside it on the floor was a brown smelly thing... a different treat. I didn't pick it up at first because by now I was aware that my condition wasn't helped by picking up strange things and eating them. I left it alone; actually turned my back on it. So mam bent down and picked it up and fed it to me from her hand. If mam was giving it to me then it must be alright I thought. It tasted okay but nowhere near as nice as the turkey. Mam fed me one of those things twice a day for the next two weeks... then they suddenly stopped. Apparently it was a course of something called concentrated pre-and-probiotics. We waited and waited for my colitis to rear its head again... but it didn't... not for a full three months... thirteen weeks and even then it was just a little episode. Mam was well chuffed but dad watched me every day for any abnormal signs... but the weeks ticked by and I began to feel magic.

\* \* \* \*

An update on the colitis. Folks, I think my ailment has gone. Maybe not for good... but for big long periods (big cheers all around). I know I'm tempting fate by saying that. I can't cross my fingers like human folk so I'm doing it with my eyes instead whilst I tell you this (I bet you're all trying to imagine a cross-eyed Westie). I haven't had a single flare up for months now; not even a sniff of one and those smelly treats have been chucked out by dad: they've gone past their use-by date or something. He's buying some more from that Amazon man. I'm still on a strict diet but I know it's for my own good and my ongoing health. Now I'm looking forward to every single day.

    That's about all from me folks. I just didn't want to be left out of dad's book. I didn't manage to get a mention in the first two volumes of his 'North-East Diaries' trilogy so I had to squeeze myself in somewhere. He's just finished the final volume of the trilogy and he's subtitled it - 'Times They are A Changing,' and I don't get a mention in that one either. Ohh aye... and by the way... I found out that dad had another dog companion when he lived in Northumberland. He'd never said anything about that to me but I heard mam laughing one day when she was going through dad's papers for him. He's a writer of stories now but he started out writing poetry a long time ago and won prizes too. He'd written a poem about his dog whom he called Nobby... named after a footballer. Anyway Mam thought it was funny. Here it is... but don't tell dad it was me who told you... and thank you all for letting me tag on to my brother's story. (Yours Faithfully – Wee Jack). Bye for now human folk.

# DAD'S POEM
# GIVE A DOG A BAD NAME

I shouldn't have called my dog 'Nobby'.
Though it seemed pretty cool at the time.
I didn't think it would hurt my dog's feelings.
And let's be honest, it isn't a crime.

We were really good pals to be truthful.
And 'Nobby' became my best friend.
We would walk in the park on an evening.
On the beach almost every weekend.

We'd play 'fetch' with a ball or a frisbee.
In summer when evenings were light.
Then he'd lay on the couch watching telly.
And on the foot of my bed every night.

My friends and my neighbours adored him.
The street kids all thought he was fun.
I taught him to fetch my newspaper.
But he refused if I asked for 'The Sun'.

And the landlord down at my local.
Thought 'Nobby' was such a delight.
He turned a blind eye to his presence.
When I played darts on Wednesday night.

Sometimes we'd go to the pub in the daytime.
And we'd chat with a lonely old dear.
Who would sit there and tickle my doggie.
Then slip him a saucer of beer.

Then we'd mosey back home together.
And search in the fridge for our tea.
Sometimes I'd give him some dog food.
And sometimes the same food as me.

Then just when life seemed so perfect.
It couldn't be better... I thought.
Fate's fickle finger soon found me.
And singled me out for some sport.

For one dull afternoon we'd been drinking.
And had a few more than was wise.
I tried walking straight, but I couldn't.
It was something to do with my eyes.

And too many saucers of lager.
Had affected my furry best friend.
He was chasing his tail in a circle.
And driving himself round the bend.

So we headed for home in a stupor.
But weren't making very good speed.
And as we passed the primary school.
He somehow escaped from his lead.

## A Westie's Song

And shot through the school gates like lightning.
Then made for a half-open door.
With a mighty great leap he was through it.
And went skidding along on the floor.

I was stumbling along well behind him.
But.......when I reached the door he was gone.
Then I heard shouts and screams from a classroom.
But I didn't know which was the one...

...That my dopey drunk mutt had invaded.
So I barged through the door that was first.
And confronted a sea of young faces.
As into their classroom I burst.

Their teacher looked fearsome and threatening.
So really she left me no choice.
**'Has anyone here seen my Nobby?'**
I screamed at the top of my voice.

They say that day wasn't my finest.
And I know that myself all too well.
And this poem that I'm writing for you.
I'm having to write from my cell.

As for 'Nobby' he lives with my mother.
While I sit here alone in the nick.
No more silly dog names in the future.
Next time..........maybe Willy or Dick?

**The Real... Real End (Honest).**

# ACKNOWLEDGEMENTS

*For all the folk who've fussed over us Westies*

Jean Macpherson & husband Mike, daughter Jennifer, Spar Sandy, Sandra Mackenzie, Alistair Will, Hector Miller, Matthew & Lindsay Fox, Ingrid Hunter, Andy Still, (Big Julian, Little Julian, June & Jonathon – chaseable posties), Maggie & Ben, The Spar Staff, Tracy & Rudi Abrams, Clare (vet nurse), Neil (vet), Jill & John Sim, Ronnie & Kitty Taylor, Shelley cuz (famous pie demolisher), Brian, Michelle & Sarah Long, Dave & Sharon Kenworthy, Joan Richardson, Jacqueline Colton, Frances McKay (Alzheimers), James and Aimee Mackay, Grant & Shannon Ross, Mike and Lesley Voge (not forgetting Aidan & Teagan and Torin of course), Erin Mackay (canny hairdresser), Helen & Brian Reid, Rae and Jan Davie.

The biggest shout out however is for Ingrid Hunter, a local amateur artist from Pitcalnie who designed the front and rear covers of this book. Many thanks and I hope to utilise your talents again.

Our next-door dogs and guests.

*Cora, Liath, Ailagh, Rolo, Rudy, Indy, Orlagh, Jodie, Jack, Tori, Pepper... not in any particular order as I forget!*

And Finally, Jack With Best Pal Torin.

A Westie's Song

# END

Printed in Great Britain
by Amazon